Four Introductory Lectures On Political Economy

By

Nassau William Senior

Four Introductory Lectures
On Political Economy
by Nassau William Senior

ISBN: 978-93-62201-53-9

Published by

DOUBLE 9 BOOKS

2/13-B, Ansari Road
Daryaganj, New Delhi – 110002
info@double9books.com
www.double9books.com
Tel. 011-40042856

ABOUT THE AUTHOR

Nassau William Senior was an English barrister and economist. He also served as a government adviser on economic and social policy for numerous decades, and he published extensively about the subject. He was born in Compton, Berkshire, as the eldest son of Reverend J. R. Senior, vicar of Durnford, Wiltshire. He attended Eton College and Magdalen College in Oxford, and while at university, he was a private pupil of Richard Whately, later Archbishop of Dublin, with whom he had a lifelong connection. He earned his B.A. in 1811 and became a Vinerian Scholar in 1813. He was born in Compton, Berkshire, as the eldest son of Reverend J. R. Senior, vicar of Durnford, Wiltshire. He attended Eton College and Magdalen College in Oxford, and while at university, he was a private pupil of Richard Whately, later Archbishop of Dublin, with whom he had a lifelong connection. He earned his B.A. in 1811 and became a Vinerian Scholar in 1813. Senior pursued a career in conveyancing after studying under Edward Burtenshaw Sugden. When Sugden abruptly notified his students in 1816 that he was focusing on chancery work, Senior took steps to become a Certified Conveyancer, which he accomplished in 1817. He then took up Sugden's practice alongside another student, Aaron Hurrill.

CONTENTS

LECTURE I
CAUSES THAT HAVE RETARDED THE PROGRESS OF POLITICAL ECONOMY

Political Economy, as a separate branch of study, may be said to be about a century old. Many of the facts which are its subject-matter, have indeed attracted human attention from the earliest times; many opinions, right or wrong, have been formed respecting them, and many customs and laws, beneficial or injurious, have been the consequence: but it was not until nearly the middle of the last century, that any attempt was made to reduce those opinions into a system, or to ascertain the grounds on which they were founded, or even how far they were reconcilable with one another. To M. Quesnay belongs the honour of having first endeavoured to explain of what wealth consists, by what means it is produced, increased, and diminished, and according to what laws distributed; in other words, of having been the first teacher of Political Economy. In the course of his investigations, he found that in the pursuit of wealth all governments had not merely mistaken the straight road, but had frequently pursued a path leading directly away from it. He found that instead of endeavouring to attain a beneficial end by appropriate measures, they had been aiming at a useless result by means totally ineffectual. Until his time it had been supposed that wealth consists of gold and silver, and that the quantity of gold and silver in any given country is to be increased by encouraging the exportation and discouraging the importation of all other commodities, and by the perpetual interference of governments in the modes in which the labour of their subjects is exerted, and the objects to which it is directed. Quesnay showed that gold and silver make the smallest and least important portion of the wealth of a country. And he showed that the abundance of gold and silver, and of every other commodity, is to be promoted, not by restrictions on importation, nor by bounties on exportation, but by the absolute freedom of external and internal trade; by securing to every man the results of his industry or frugality, without attempting to order him what to produce or how to enjoy.

His inquiries seem to have produced on his own mind, and on the minds of his disciples, effects resembling those which would be created by the discovery of a map by a party who had been long wandering in an imperfectly known country. His map, indeed, was often inaccurate, but the points in which it was correct were the most important, and its errors, such as they were, were not detected by those to whom he offered it. Few men have ever presented to the human mind a more interesting subject of inquiry, and few have had a more devoted band of disciples. La Riviere, Mirabeau, Turgot, and the other writers forming the school called the French Economists, all implicitly adopted Quesnay's opinions, and engaged zealously in their propagation.

The inquiry which Quesnay originated was pursued, and with still greater success, by Adam Smith. Smith was superior to Quesnay, and perhaps to every writer since the times of Aristotle, in the extent and accuracy of his knowledge. He was, on the whole, as original a thinker as Quesnay, without being equally subject to the common defect of original thinkers, a tendency to push his favourite theories to extremes; and in the far greater freedom then allowed to industry in Great Britain than in France, and in the greater publicity with us of the government receipt and expenditure, he possessed far greater advantages as an observer. With these high qualifications and favourable opportunities, and assisted by a style unequalled in its attractiveness, he has almost completely superseded the labours of his predecessors. The few who read their writings, read them not in the hope of obtaining the instruction which they were intended to afford, but as sources of historical information, or as examples of the errors to which powerful minds may be subject in the infancy of a study.

From the appearance of the "Wealth of Nations," Political Economy has excited a constantly increasing interest. All the events, fortunate and unfortunate, which have occurred in Europe during that extraordinary period, have tended both to increase its actual importance, and to occasion that importance to be better estimated. The art to which it is principally applicable is the great art of government, and particularly that branch of government which consists in the raising and employment of public money. Not a tax can be imposed or applied without materially affecting the fortunes of those by whom it is paid, of those among whom it is expended, and of third persons, many of whom, perhaps, are unaware of its existence. To ascertain the character and the extent of these effects, even as to any existing tax, without the aid of the general principles supplied by Political Economy, is scarcely practicable: to foretell or even to conjecture, with probability, the effects of an untried tax, without such aid, is impossible. A government ignorant of the nature of wealth, or of the laws which regulate its production and distribution, resembles a surgeon who has not studied anatomy, or a judge unacquainted with law.

But, under the old system of Continental Europe, many things concurred to diminish the attention which the evil consequences of this ignorance might have been expected to attract. Each monarchy was considered the patrimony of its king, and its public revenue a portion of his income. All that he could get he spent or gave away; part of it went in wars for his honour, part was wasted in building and pageantry, and part was distributed among his courtiers. Public debts were few and small, and were the debts, not of the nation, but of the crown. The interest was not an additional burden on the people, but a deduction from the gratifications of the prince, and was reduced from time to time, either by depreciating the currency, or by the simple expedient of a refusal to pay. No right was recognised in the public to inquire into the amount of the royal revenue, the sources from which it was derived, or the purposes to which it was applied. These were the private affairs of the sovereign, which it was not decent or even safe to canvass.

All this was changed at once by the French Revolution. It was proclaimed in France, and admitted, or scarcely denied, on the rest of the Continent, that governments are made for nations, not nations for governments; and that the public revenue is the revenue, not of the government, but of the nation, — not a property, but a trust, — not a rent or a tribute, but the purchase-money of the labour necessary to prevent foreign and domestic violence and fraud, paid over to the government merely as an administrator, unlawfully employed if applied to any other purpose, and unlawfully demanded if more than necessary for that purpose.

Every man felt himself interested that the proportion of his income which he had to pay over to the state should be reduced, either by diminishing expenditure, or by varying the mode of assessment.

At the same time the wars in which Europe was involved for a quarter of a century, and the scale on which they were carried on, occasioned in almost every country an enormous increase of that proportion of the whole income of the people which is administered by the government. Almost every country created a national debt, and thus threw on its rulers the additional duty of collecting a revenue, to be applied, not for current expenses, but to repay those who had advanced the public expenditure of previous years. And not only were the people induced to interest themselves in public affairs, they were frequently called upon to act. In many countries the whole form of government was more than once demolished and reconstructed. Almost every nation, at some period, received, or was promised, representative institutions; everywhere the monarch, by appealing to the people, recognised the existence and the force of a national will.

In the British Islands self-government was no novelty, but many circumstances concurred to increase and diffuse the interest taken in public affairs. Among these circumstances the principal ones were the extension of the public expenditure, the alterations in the currency, and the effects of the poor laws. In no extensive empire recorded in history, has so large a portion of the annual produce of the land, labour, and capital of the people, been administered by the state. Every man felt himself to be a public debtor, and almost every man became, in some shape or other, a public creditor. At the same time the nominal value of money, the standard by which his claims and liabilities were measured, was subject to variations considerable in themselves, grossly exaggerated by one party, and absolutely denied by another, of which few could point out the immediate causes, and no one could foretell the probable extent. Meanwhile, the effects of the poor laws over the southern and south-eastern districts of England, became every day more apparent. It became obvious to the most unreflecting, that they were gradually altering the rights, both of property and of industry, the relations between the poor and the rich, the labourer and his employer, and the habits and feelings of the agricultural, and in many places of the town population.

All these causes, and many others which it would be tedious and almost impossible to enumerate, have given to the political sciences, during the last sixty years, an interest which no study, except perhaps that of theology during the early progress of the Reformation, ever acquired. And this at a period when the extension of books and newspapers, and of the habits and means of discussion and communication, has been such as our most sanguine ancestors never anticipated.

Of all the branches of political knowledge, the most important, and the most applicable to the purposes of government, is that which considers the nature and the origin of wealth. It is true that the ultimate object of government, and indeed the ultimate object of every individual, is happiness. But we know that the means by which almost every man endeavours to increase his happiness, or, to use the common phrase, to better his condition, is by increasing his wealth. And to assist, or rather to protect him in doing this, is the great difficulty in government. All the fraud, and almost all the violence, for the prevention of which government is submitted to, arise from the attempts of mankind to deprive one another of the fruits of their respective industry and frugality. To counteract these attempts, a public revenue must be raised and expended; and, as I have already remarked, neither of these operations can be well executed or well judged of by persons ignorant of Political Economy. It may be added, that the desire for unjust gain, which, among savages, produces robbery and theft, assumes, among civilised nations, the less palpable forms of monopoly, combination, and privilege; abuses which, when of long standing, it requires much knowledge of general principles to detect or expose, and which it is still more difficult to remedy without occasioning much immediate injury to individuals.

I think, therefore, that I may venture to say, that no study ever attracted, during an equal period, so much attention from so many minds, as has been bestowed, during the last sixty years, on Political Economy. I do not mean that this attention was acknowledged, or even that all those who have been framing and repeating theories respecting the modes in which wealth is created, increased, or diminished, have been aware that they were political economists. Most of them as little suspected it as M. Jourdain that he was speaking prose. But every country gentleman who has demanded protection to agriculture, every manufacturer who has deprecated free trade, every speculator who has called for paper currency, every one who has attacked, and almost every one who has defended, the measures of the minister for the time being, has drawn his principal arguments from Political Economy.

At the same time, the avowed writers on this subject have been more numerous than those on any other science or art. If we look at our principal reviews, we shall find that a large portion of each number is dedicated to it. M. Say has been translated over and over, into every language in Europe. I have seen three different translations of his great work published in different parts of Spain. In the United States of America there are newspapers exclusively devoted to it, and it has professors in almost every university in Europe, and in North America.

Has then, I will ask,—and it was as an introduction to these questions that I have ventured on so long a preface,—has the progress of Political Economy been in proportion to the ardour with which it has been urged? If it has not been so, by what causes has its progress been retarded? and are they causes within our control?

To the first question, the answer must be, No. After so much and so long continued discussion, we might have hoped that its limits would have been accurately laid down, its terms defined, and its general principles admitted. It is unnecessary to prove formally that this is not the case. Every one is aware that Political Economy is in a state of imperfect development,—I will not say characteristic of infancy, but certainly very far from maturity. We seldom hear its principles made the subject of conversation, without perceiving that each interlocutor has his own theory as to the objects to which the inquiries of a political economist ought to be directed, and the mode in which they ought to be pursued. When we read the most eminent of the recent writers on the subject, we find them chiefly engaged in controversy. Instead of being able to use the works of his fellow labourers, every economist begins by demolition, and erects an edifice, resting perhaps, in a great measure, on the same foundations, but differing from all that has preceded it in form and arrangement.

Supposing it to be conceded that this is a correct representation of the actual situation of the study, I proceed to the more important questions, by what obstacles has its improvement been impeded, and are there any, and what means, by which they may be removed?

One of the principal causes which has prevented the progress of Political Economy from being adequate to the attention which has been bestowed on it, is inherent in its nature. I will not say unfortunately so, since it is at the same time the principal cause of the attention which it deserves, and, in fact, of the attention which it has received. I mean its direct influence on the welfare of mankind; and the effect on our reasonings of this disturbing cause, has been strikingly increased by the state of transition in which the institutions of almost all the civilised world have been struggling for the last sixty years, and seem destined to struggle for an indefinite period.

If our laws had been of the unchangeable character which has been ascribed to those of the Medes and Persians, we might have investigated the nature and sources of wealth with the impartiality with which we study the motions of the heavenly bodies. No one would have felt himself interested in denying conclusions which would have been unsusceptible of practical application. That wealth consists, not of money, but of the things which money can purchase,—that it is not lessened by resorting to the cheapest market,—that it is not augmented by augmenting the nominal value of the tokens by which it is measured,—that it increases with the increasing productiveness of labour, and diminishes if more labour be required to produce a given result,—that the profits of commerce consist not in what is given, but in what is received, are propositions which might have been neglected as truisms, or alluded to as self-evident, but could scarcely have been made the subjects of eager controversy. Monopolies would never have been defended, if monopolists had been secure.

It is to the difference in this respect in the state of Europe, that I ascribe the difference in the degree of clamour which was raised against Adam Smith in England, and the earlier economists in France, and that which has been directed against their successors in both countries. The doctrines of Quesnay and Smith were as much opposed to existing abuses as those of Malthus or of Ricardo; but there did not appear to be the same chance of their application. While restriction and prohibition was the rule, and apparently the unalterable rule, political economists were forgiven for proclaiming the advantages of free trade. The theory was even admitted as long as the practice seemed at a distance. But these halcyon times are over: it is becoming every day more apparent, that whatever is generally believed to be expedient, will sooner or later be attempted; and that institutions are to be attacked and defended, not by force, but by argument,—not by mere clamour, or dogged refusal, but by convincing the public of the benefit or of the disadvantage of the proposed alteration.

Archbishop Whately has well remarked, that the demonstrations of Euclid would not have commanded universal assent, if they had been applicable to the pursuits and fortunes of individuals; and of all branches of human knowledge, Political Economy, from the complexity of its relations, and the vagueness of its nomenclature, offers the easiest scope to a prejudiced or an uncandid reasoner. The great improvements that are taking place in our commercial and financial policy, will tend to diminish this obstacle to political science by removing the subjects of contest. And we may hope that its force will be still further diminished by the mere progress of the study, as its terms become better defined, and more and more of its principles are established and recognised. But it would be vain to hope that it ever will be got rid of, or that men will examine questions which come home to their business and bosoms, with the unbiassed spirit which urges the astronomer or the mathematician.

Another cause which has rendered fruitless much of the attention bestowed on Political Economy, has been the frequent attempt to discuss insulated questions connected with it, by those who have not previously endeavoured to acquaint themselves with its general outline. In some sciences this is, to a certain extent, practicable. In those sciences which consist in a great measure of independent facts, such as law, or natural history, a single branch may sometimes be studied successfully. But in Political Economy the different propositions are so mutually dependent, that it is impossible to reason safely concerning any one without constantly bearing in mind all the others. And yet nothing is more common than to find persons writing books and making speeches, and even proposing, with the utmost confidence, legislative measures involving principles as to which the acutest and most diligent inquirer has not been able to make up his mind, not only without having settled within themselves the meaning of their principal terms, but even without being themselves aware that they are using words to which they attach no definite ideas.

The errors which I have mentioned have been committed principally by those who, without being professedly political economists, frequently indeed expressly disclaiming that character, have treated the subjects which Political Economy considers. But many who have avowedly devoted themselves to its pursuit, seem to have misdirected their efforts, for want of a clear conception of the object of their investigations, of the manner in which they ought to be conducted, or of the nature of the difficulties to be surmounted. If the teacher of Political Economy has not decided whether he is engaged on a science or on an art, whether it is his duty to explain phenomena or to deliver precepts, whether his principal business is to observe facts or to deduce inferences, whether his premises are all physical truths or depend partly on arbitrary assumption,—his work, though it may contain partial views of the highest value, cannot possibly form a clear or a consistent whole. Nor is it sufficient that the professor should have made up his mind as to what he has to teach. It is important, though not equally important, that the student should have a general notion as to what he has to learn, as to the nature of the subjects which are to be laid before him, of the conclusions to which he will be asked to assent, and of the arguments by which they will be supported. The view that is to be taken, may perhaps not suit his habits of thought or of inquiry. It may be too abstract or too concrete. If he be accustomed to demonstration, he may be ill satisfied by proofs and illustrations drawn from actual life, and mixed with irrelevant accidents. If his pursuits have been practical, he may be disgusted by reasonings founded on hypotheses representing nothing that actually takes place. Or his objections may be directed rather against the subject itself than against the mode of its treatment. He may think that too much importance, or if not too much importance, too exclusive an attention, is directed towards wealth. He may wish that economists would consider man as a being with higher qualities, higher duties, and higher enjoyments than those which are concerned in the production, distribution, and consumption of commodities and services, and may regret to see him treated merely as a cause or a recipient of rents, profits, and wages. But if he be forewarned, he will not be disappointed, and, knowing beforehand the sort of study in which he is to be engaged, he will more easily perceive the premises and weigh the arguments of its professor.

LECTURE II
POLITICAL ECONOMY A MENTAL STUDY

In the present and the following two Lectures, I shall consider whether Political Economy is a physical or a mental study; whether it may be more conveniently treated as a science or as an art; and whether its premises are to be taken solely from observation and consciousness, or rest, in part, on arbitrary assumptions. And I shall begin by stating, at some length, the distinction between science and art,—not with the hope of saying anything new, but because I believe that that distinction, though it has been clearly drawn, may not be familiar to all my hearers.

Shortly, it may be said that, as a history is a statement of past facts, so a science is a statement of existing facts, and an art a statement of the means by which future facts may be caused or influenced, or, in other words, future events brought about. The first two aim only at supplying materials for the memory and the judgment; they do not presuppose any purpose beyond the acquisition of knowledge. The third is intended to influence the will. It presupposes that some object is to be attained, and points out the easiest, the safest, or the most effectual conduct for that purpose. It is for this reason that the collection of related facts which constitute a science is generally a less complex thing than the collection of related precepts which constitute an art. A single science may be complete in itself;—a man may confine himself to chemistry, or to zoology, or to botany. He may pursue any one of those sciences to the boundaries of existing knowledge, and know nothing of the others. But an art must draw its materials from many sciences. No man can teach or practise well the art of agriculture unless he have some knowledge of chemistry, botany, zoology, mechanics, and indeed of many other sciences.

In the progress of human knowledge art precedes science. The first efforts of man are practical. He has an object in view, and tries various means of accomplishing it. Some of these utterly fail, some succeed imperfectly, and others are effectual, but at an unnecessary expense of time and trouble. As his experience increases, he gradually lays down for himself certain practical rules. If the business in which he is engaged can be managed by a solitary individual, these rules may be known only to himself, and be lost at his death. It is thus that we have lost many of the secrets of the ancient painters. But if it be one that requires co-operation, they become known to his assistants and to his pupils, and gradually to all who are engaged in similar pursuits. Many minds are employed in improving them and in adding to their number, until at length they swell into a system. It may be long, however, before they exist in any but a traditional form. The great architects of the middle ages left behind them no written precepts. They taught their pupils by oral instruction, and the rest of the world and posterity by example. The desire, however, to communicate and perpetuate information is one of the strongest passions of inventive minds. As books multiply and become the principal means by which this can be effected, those who are conscious of superior knowledge become writers. They compose treatises in which the means which are supposed to be productive of certain effects are arranged and preserved; and the knowledge which previously rested on individual experience or traditional routine becomes an art.

With the exception, however, of poetry, architecture, and generally of the arts that are addressed to the taste and the imagination, for which nations in an early stage of civilisation seem to have a peculiar aptitude, the arts of an unscientific age contain many rules ineffectual for their intended purposes, and many that are positively opposed to them. Thus the medicine of the middle ages ordered plants with yellow flowers to be used in cases of jaundice, and those with red flowers in fevers, and directed fomentations and ointments to be applied not to the wound but to the sword. At length a man arrives with wider views or less docile habits of mind, who is not satisfied to obey what often appear to him to be arbitrary rules, though he is told that they are the results of experience. He endeavours to account for the effects which he sees produced, that is to say, to refer them to some general laws of matter or of mind. To do this is to create a science. As soon as scientific habits of thought prevail, men are teazed by any appearance for which they cannot account. Their first motive is to question its reality. Evidence of mesmeric clairvoyance has been produced enough to satisfy a sceptical inquirer, if the phenomenon itself could be accounted for. But we cannot refer it to any general law, and therefore the greater part of those who think about it, deny its existence; many suspend their opinion, and scarcely any are complete believers. If its existence should ever be thoroughly established, the whole scientific world will be engaged in searching for the general principles to which it is to be referred; for no one will be satisfied with accepting it as an insulated unexplained fact.

I have said that a single art generally draws its premises from many different sciences. So a single science generally affords premises to many different arts. How numerous are the sciences which are applicable to the art of war. How numerous are the arts which depend in part on the principles of chemistry. And it is obvious that every increase of human knowledge must increase the influence of science on art. Under this influence many new rules are laid down, and many, which were supposed to be founded on experience, are abandoned as unnecessary or injurious. The art becomes in some respects more simple and in others more complex: more complex because its precepts become more diversified and more detailed; more simple because, instead of being thrown together with little apparent connection, they are grouped under the general principles supplied by science.

Sciences are divided into two great classes, differing both as to the matters which they treat, and the sources from which they draw their premises. These are the physical and the mental, or, as they are sometimes called, the moral sciences. The proper subjects of the first are the properties of matter; those of the second are the sensations, faculties, and habits of the human mind. As we have no experience of mind separated from matter (perhaps indeed are incapable of conceiving its existence), and as the mind can act only through the body, even the more purely mental sciences are forced to take notice of matter; and many of them, such as the sciences which have been called æsthetic, those which account for the pleasure which we derive from beauty and sublimity, seem at first sight to treat of little except material objects. But they consider those objects merely with reference to their effects on the human mind. To classify and account for those effects as a part of the philosophy of mind is the purpose of the science, and it regards in matter only the qualities which produce them. On the other hand, a botanist in the description of plants cannot omit the qualities which render them agreeable or useful to man. Without doubt, to be pleased by the sight and smell of a rose is as much an attribute of the human mind as the form, colour, and other qualities which occasion that pleasure are attributes of the rose. But it is to the rose only that the botanist looks. He states that it is beautiful and odoriferous as a part of the description of the plant, not of that of the being to whom it is beautiful and odoriferous.

The same difference separates arts, though the line is less clearly marked. For as every art must use material instruments, it is to a certain extent physical; and as every art aims at producing pleasure or preventing pain, it must be, to a certain extent, mental. Still, however, the difference exists. No one would call rhetoric a physical art, though its teacher must deliver precepts as to voice and gesture. No one would call agriculture a mental art, though a treatise on agriculture would be incomplete which did not compare the advantages and disadvantages of task-work and day-work,—a comparison involving wide and numerous moral considerations.

Where the subject is matter the distinction between an art and a science is in general easily perceptible. No one confounds the science of projectiles with the art of gunnery, or the art of surgery with the science of anatomy. But it appears to be much less easy to distinguish the arts and the sciences which have for their subject the operations of the human mind. Thus we often talk of the art of logic, and of the science of morality. But logic is not an art but a science. It is not a collection of precepts how to reason, but a statement of the principles on which all reasoning depends. The logician does not advise, he merely instructs. He does not teach us to argue by means of syllogisms, but asserts the fact that all reasoning is syllogistic. His statements are all general; they have no relation to time or to place. They are unconnected with any science but his own. On the other hand, morality is not a science but an art. The object of the moralist is not to inform us as to the nature of the faculties and the sensations of man, but to advise us how to use those faculties, and how to subject ourselves to those sensations, for the purpose of promoting our happiness. He must therefore draw his materials from many different sciences, and must vary his precepts according to the social condition of those whom he addresses. The morality of the Stoics was fitted to an aggregate of petty communities constantly engaged in foreign and civil war, in which defeat involved the worst of human evils, the loss of life, of relations, of property, and of liberty. No Greek could be sure that in a year's time his country might not be conquered by a neighbouring tribe, or his party overthrown by a revolution, and all his family and friends murdered before his eyes, or sold with him into slavery. Under such circumstances, insensibility, the power of enduring the approach and the presence of evil, and the insecurity, and even the absence of good, appeared to be the quality most conducive to happiness. The Stoic moralist, therefore, was as anxious to blunt the desires and harden the perceptions of his pupils, as the English moralist is to rouse their ambition, and to expand their sensibility. The logic of Aristotle and the logic of Whately are the same, but how little do we find in common when we compare the morality of Zeno with that of Smith or of Paley.

It appears to me that the greater tendency to confound science and art, when the subject is mind, than when it is matter, arises from the more immediate influence on human conduct possessed by the mental sciences. The sciences which consider matter have often little apparent connection with any of the arts to which they are subservient. The application of chemistry to agriculture has taken place almost within our own recollection; its application to navigation is still more recent; to transport by land, more recent still; to the transmission of intelligence, scarcely ten years old. Such sciences may be, and indeed generally are, most earnestly studied by men who have no object beyond the discovery and diffusion of truth. That object is enough to satisfy the most ardent scientific ambition, and to urge the most unwearied scientific labours. The astronomer does not consider what will be the practical results of his inquiries, or whether they will lead to any practical results whatever. His object is knowledge. The uses to which that knowledge may be applied, the mode and the degree in which it may affect men's conduct, he leaves to others.

On the other hand, the mental sciences are directly and obviously connected with the arts of which they furnish the principles; and those arts almost every educated man must practise. No man studies the science of reasoning without resolving to apply its principles whenever he has to exercise the art of controversy. No man inquires into the laws which regulate the human intellect or the human passions, without framing out of them some practical rules for the employment of his own faculties and the regulation of his own affections.

The distinction between physical and mental is important, not only with respect to the subjects treated by the sciences and arts in each class, but also with respect to the principal sources from which they respectively draw their premises.

In all sciences and in all arts these sources are but three—observation, consciousness, and hypothesis. The physical sciences, being only secondarily conversant with mind, draw their premises almost exclusively from observation or hypothesis. Those which treat only of magnitude and number, or, as they are usually called, the pure sciences, draw them altogether from hypothesis. The mathematician does not measure the radii of a circle in order to ascertain that they are all equal: he infers their equality from the definition with which he sets out. Those which abstain from hypothesis depend on observation. It is by observation that the astronomer ascertains the motions of the planets, the botanist classifies plants, and the chemist discovers the affinities of different bodies. They disregard almost entirely the phenomena of consciousness. The physical *arts* are almost exclusively based on observation. As their object is to produce positive effects, they trust as little as possible to hypothesis; and the mental phenomena which they have to consider are generally few and simple. The art of navigation, the art of mining, or the art of fortification, might be taught by a man who had never studied seriously the operations of his own mind.

On the other hand, the mental sciences and the mental arts draw their premises principally from consciousness. The subjects with which they are chiefly conversant are the workings of the human mind. And the only mind whose workings a man really knows is his own. When he wishes to ascertain the thoughts and the feelings of others, his first impulse always is, to endeavour to suppose himself in what he believes to be their situation, and to consider how he himself would then think and feel. His next impulse is to infer that similar moral and intellectual processes are taking place in them. If he be a cautious observer, he endeavours to correct this inference by examining their countenances, their words, and their actions. But these are uncertain symptoms, often occasioned by a state of mind different from that which they appear to indicate; and often employed for the purpose of concealment or of deception.

When a man endeavours to discover what is passing in the mind of another, by reflecting on what has passed or is passing in his own, the certainty of the result depends of course on the degree in which the two minds coincide. The educated man, therefore, estimates ill the feelings and the faculties of the uneducated, the adult those of the child, the sane those of the insane, the civilised man those of the savage. And this accounts for the constant mismanagement of the lower orders, and of children, madmen, and savages, by their intellectual and moral superiors. The student of mental science is in the situation of an anatomist, allowed to dissect only a single subject, and forced to conjecture the internal conformation of other men by assuming that it resembles that of the subject which he has dissected, and correcting that assumption only by observing the forms of their bones and the outward play of their muscles. The mental peculiarities of other men are likely to mislead him in particular instances. His own mental peculiarities are likely to mislead him on all occasions.

Another important difference, between mental and physical studies, is the degree and the manner in which they respectively can be aided by experiment. When we are dealing with matter, we frequently are able to combine its particles at will, and to ascertain the results of the combination. If we find that, all other things remaining the same, the presence or absence of a given element is followed by the presence or absence of a given result, we ascribe to that element and to that result the relation of cause and effect, or at least of condition and result.

But we can scarcely be said to be able to make experiments on the minds of others. It is necessary to an experiment, that the observer should know accurately the state of the thing observed before the experiment, and its state immediately after it. But when the minds of other men are the subject, we can know but little of either the one state or of the other. We are forced, therefore, to rely not on experiment, but on experience, that is to say, not on combinations of known elements effected for the purpose of testing the result of each different combination, but on our observation of actual occurrences, the results of the combination of numerous elements, only a few of which are within our own knowledge. And the consequence is, that we frequently connect facts which are really independent of one another, and not unfrequently mistake obstacles for causes.

The measure now[A] before parliament for introducing into Ireland a compulsory provision for the destitute, is defended by an appeal to experience. We are told that the English poor have such a provision, and are the most industrious and the best maintained population in Europe. The Irish poor have no such provision, and are the idlest and the poorest people that is called civilised. If the presence of a poor law in the one and its absence in the other were the only difference in the history of the two countries, this would really be an instance of experience. If a country with a previous history precisely resembling that of England, possessing precisely the same physical and moral advantages, and differing solely in the absence of a poor law, were found to be idle and miserable, we might justly infer that the prosperity of England is owing to its poor law; for there would be no other cause to which it could be referred. And the misery of the other country could be referred to no cause except its want of a poor law. But when we find that the English and the Irish nations differ in race, in religion, and in habits,—that the one is chiefly a town and the other almost exclusively a country population,—that the one consists principally of labourers for hire, the other of small tenants,—that the one lives on wages, the other on its own crop,—that the vice of the one is improvidence, that of the other indolence,— that in one country the religion of the people has been persecuted, in the other endowed,—that in the one the clergy of the people are the allies of the government, in the other its enemies,—that in the one public sympathy is with the supporter of order and peace, in the other with the disturber,— that the code which prevails in the one is that which is sanctioned by parliament and administered by courts of justice, in the other is one framed by conspirators, promulgated by threatening notices, and enforced by outrage and assassination,—that it is more dangerous to obey the law in the one than to violate it in the other,—when we find that these differences have lasted for centuries, and that, almost from our earliest knowledge of them, the circumstances in which the two countries have been placed have been not only dissimilar but opposed, it is obvious that the wretchedness of Ireland in the absence of a poor law does not prove that the presence of such an institution has been beneficial to England. All that is proved is that a country can prosper with a poor law and be miserable without one. To that extent the experience of England and Ireland is decisive. It is a complete answer to any one who should maintain either that a country in which the population are forced to rely for subsistence on their own resources will necessarily be laborious, or that one in which the law protects every one, whatever be his conduct, from want, will necessarily be indolent. But it is no answer to any one who should maintain that such are the tendencies of the two opposite institutions, but that such tendencies may be neutralised by counteracting causes. And yet there are thousands of educated men who call such reasoning as this arguing from experience, and are now anxious to make the tremendous experiment of an Irish poor law on the English model in reliance on what they call the experience of England.

[A] This Lecture was delivered in March, 1847.

When we direct our attention to the workings of our own minds, that is to say, when we search for premises by means of consciousness instead of by means of observation, our powers of trying experiments are much greater. To a considerable degree we command our own faculties, and though there are few, perhaps none, which we can use separately, we can at will exercise one more vigorously than the others. We can call, for instance, into peculiar activity, the judgment, the memory, or the imagination, and note the differences in our mental condition as the one faculty or the other is more active. And this is an experiment. Over our mental sensations we have less power. We cannot at will feel angry, or envious, or frightened. But we can sometimes, though rarely, put ourselves really into situations by which certain emotions will be excited. And when, as is usually the case, this is impossible or objectionable, we can fancy ourselves in such situations. The first is an actual experiment. We can approach the brink of an unprotected precipice and look down. We can interpose between our bodies and that brink a low parapet, and look over it. And if we find that our emotions in the two cases differ,—that though there is no real danger in either case, though in both our judgment equally tells us that we are safe, yet that the apparent danger in the one produces fear, while we feel secure in the other,—we infer that the imagination can excite fear for which the judgment affirms that there is no adequate cause. The second is the resemblance of an experiment, and when tried by a person with the vivid imagination of Shakspeare or Homer may almost serve for one. But with ordinary minds it is a most fallacious expedient. Few men when they picture themselves in an imaginary situation take into account all the incidents necessary to that situation. And those which they neglect may be among the most important.

Having explained the distinction between a science and an art, and the chief differences between the arts and sciences which consider as their principal subject the laws of matter, and those whose principal subject is mind, I now come to one of the practical questions in which this long preface will I hope be found useful, namely, whether Political Economy be a mental or a physical study.

Unquestionably the political economist has much to do with matter. The phenomena attending the production of material wealth occupy a great part of his attention; and these depend mainly on the laws of matter. The efficacy of machinery, the diminishing productiveness, under certain circumstances, of successive applications of capital to land, and the fecundity and longevity of the human species, are all important premises in Political Economy, and all are laws of matter. But the political economist dwells on them only with reference to the mental phenomena which they serve to explain; he considers them as among the motives to the accumulation of capital, as among the sources of rent, as among the regulators of profit, and as among the causes which promote or retard the pressure of population on subsistence. If the main subject of his studies were the physical phenomena attending the production of wealth, a system of Political Economy must contain a treatise on mechanics, on navigation, on agriculture, on chemistry—in fact, on the subjects of almost all the physical sciences and arts, for there are few of those arts or sciences which are not subservient to wealth. All these details, however, the political economist avoids, or uses a few of them sparingly for the purpose of illustration. He does not attempt to state the mechanical and chemical laws which enable the steam engine to perform its miracles—he passes them by as laws of matter; but he explains, as fully as his knowledge will allow, the motives which induce the mechanist to erect the steam engine, and the labourer to work it. And these are laws of mind. He leaves to the geologist to explain the laws of matter which occasion the formation of coal, to the chemist to distinguish its component elements, to the engineer to state the means by which it is extracted, and to the teachers of many hundred different arts to point out the uses to which it may be applied. What he reserves to himself is to explain the laws of mind under which the owner of the soil allows his pastures to be laid waste, and the minerals which they cover to be abstracted; under which the capitalist employs, in sinking shafts and piercing galleries, funds which might be devoted to his own immediate enjoyment; under which the miner encounters the toils and the dangers of his hazardous and laborious occupation; and the laws, also laws of mind, which decide in what proportions the produce, or the value of the produce, is divided between the three classes by whose concurrence it has been obtained. When he uses as his premises, as he often must do, facts supplied by physical science, he does not attempt to account for them; he is satisfied with stating their existence. If he has to prove it, he looks for his proofs, so far as he can, in the human mind. Thus the economist need not explain why it is that labour cannot be applied to a given extent of land to an indefinite amount with a proportionate return. He has done enough when he has proved that such is the fact; and he proves this by showing, on the principles of human nature, that, if it were otherwise, no land except that which is most fertile, and best situated, would be cultivated. All the technical terms, therefore, of Political Economy, represent either purely mental ideas, such as *demand, utility, value,* and *abstinence,* or objects which, though some of them may be material, are considered by the political economist so far only as they are the results or the causes of certain affections of the human mind, such as *wealth, capital, rent, wages,* and *profits.*

In the next Lecture I shall consider the first of the two remaining questions,—namely, whether Political Economy may be better treated as a science or as an art.

LECTURE III
REASONS FOR TREATING POLITICAL ECONOMY AS A SCIENCE

In the following Lecture I shall consider whether Political Economy may be better treated as a science or as an art.

If Political Economy is to be treated as a science, it may be defined as "the science which states the laws regulating the production and distribution of wealth, so far as they depend on the action of the human mind."

If it be treated as an art, it may be defined as "the art which points out the institutions and habits most conducive to the production and accumulation of wealth." Or if the teacher venture to take a wider view, as "the art which points out the institutions and habits most conducive to that production, accumulation, and distribution of wealth, which is most favourable to the happiness of mankind."

According to the law which I have already mentioned, as regulating the progress of knowledge, Political Economy, when, in the 17th century, it first attracted notice as a subject of separate study, was treated as an art. At that time human happiness was considered as dependent chiefly on wealth, and wealth, as I have previously remarked, was supposed to consist of gold and silver. The object which the political economist proposed to himself and to his reader, was the accumulation within his own country of the utmost possible amount of the precious metals. The questions which now agitate society, as to the distribution of wealth, were unregarded. All that was aimed at, was its acquisition and retention in a metallic form. As respects the countries possessing native deposits of the precious metals, the means of effecting this were supposed to be obvious and easy. They had only to promote the extraction of silver from mines, and that of gold from auriferous sands, and to prohibit the exportation of either. This was the policy of Spain and Portugal. The countries not possessing a native supply, could obtain it only by what was called a favourable balance of trade, that is to say, by exporting to a value exceeding that of their imports, and receiving the difference in money. And the money so acquired, they were taught to retain, by prohibiting its exportation. The prevailing opinion shows itself in the preamble of the 5 Rich. II. stat. 1. cap. 2., one among the many statutes and proclamations by which this prohibition was for centuries enforced. "For the great mischief which this realm suffereth, and long hath done, for that gold and silver are carried out of the realm, so that, in effect, there is none thereof left, which thing, if it should longer be suffered, would shortly be the destruction of the same realm, which God prohibit;" and the statute proceeds to forbid such exportation on pain of forfeiture. The merchants, however, who were necessarily the first to test the effects of this prohibition, found it inconvenient. Some trades, particularly those with the East, could be carried on only by the constant exportation of gold or silver, and in all others it was occasionally useful. They did not venture to attack the theory that the prosperity of a country depends on its accumulation of money. Few of them, probably, doubted its truth. But they maintained that the means by which the legislature endeavoured to promote this excellent result, in fact defeated it. "Allow us," they said, "to send out silver to Asia, and we will bring back silks and calicos, not for our own consumption, which of course would be a loss, but to sell on the Continent for more silver than they cost, and we shall add annually to the national treasure." This was assented to, and after more than four centuries of prohibition, the export of bullion was allowed by the 15 Car. II. cap. 17. "Forasmuch," says the act, "as several considerable foreign trades cannot be conveniently driven without the species of money and bullion, and that it is found, by experience, that the species of money and bullion are carried in greatest abundance, as to a common market, to such places as give free liberty of exporting the same, *and the better to keep in and increase the current coins of this kingdom*, be it enacted, that it shall be lawful to export all sorts of foreign coin and bullion, first entering the same at the custom-house."

The art of Political Economy now became more complex. Its object, indeed, was a very simple one, merely to increase the current coin of the country; but this was to be effected, not by restraining every trade which carried out bullion, but only those which carried out more than they brought in. But how were such trades to be detected? A test was supposed to be applied, by ascertaining whether their imports were intended for home consumption, or for re-exportation. In the former case, the trade, whether profitable or not to the merchant, was obviously mischievous to the country.

In the second case the trade, if profitable to the merchant, must also benefit the country, as it would receive more money than it sent out. "It is not," says Sir James Stewart[B], "by the importation of foreign commodities, and by the exportation of gold and silver, that a nation becomes poor; it is by consuming those commodities when imported. The moment the consumption begins, the balance turns. Nations which trade to India by sending out gold and silver for a return of superfluities of a most consumable nature, the consumption of which they prohibit at home, do not spend their own specie, but that of their neighbours, who purchase the returns of it for their own consumption. Consequently a nation may become immensely rich by the constant exportation of specie and importation of consumable commodities. But she would do well to beware not to resemble the milliner who took it into her head to wear the fine laces which she used to make up for her customers. While a favourable balance is preserved upon foreign trade, a nation grows richer daily; and when one nation grows richer, others must be growing poorer."

[B] An Inquiry into the Principles of Political Economy, book ii. ch. xxix. pp. 418, 419, and 422.

Sir James Stewart's work was published in 1767, and as he says that it was the work of eighteen years, it must have been written between that year and the year 1749. Though he calls Political Economy a science, he treats it as an art, and has the merit of having first given to it limits clearly separating it from the other moral and political arts. "Its object is," he says, "to secure a certain fund of subsistence for all the inhabitants, to obviate every circumstance which may render it precarious, to provide every thing necessary for supplying the wants of the society, and to employ the inhabitants in such a manner as naturally to create reciprocal relations and dependencies between them, so as to make their several interests lead them to supply one another with their reciprocal wants."[C] This agrees with my second proposal, namely, to define Political Economy as "the art which points out the institutions and habits most conducive to the production and accumulation of wealth." As incidental to the art, he was forced to examine the science, and a considerable portion of his work consists of inquiries into the laws which regulate the production and distribution of wealth. The extracts which I have read, show that he did not escape the prevalent errors of his times. And these errors were so grave, as to render the practical portion of his treatise not merely useless for its intended purposes, but positively injurious. A legislator following his precepts, would waste the wealth of the richest country, and destroy the diligence of the most industrious. But the scientific part of the work, particularly the chapters on population, and on the influence of taxation on wages, contains truths of great importance, which were unknown to his contemporaries, and cannot be said to be generally recognised even now.

[C] Book I. Introduction.

Among the contemporaries of Stewart were the French Economists, or, as they have lately been called, the Physiocrats, forming the school founded by Quesnay. With the exception, however, of Turgot, they wrote on the whole art of government. Their works, indeed, contain treatises on Political Economy according to my third proposed definition, that is to say, "on the institutions and habits most conducive to that production, accumulation, and distribution of wealth, which is most favourable to the happiness of mankind;" but they contain much more. Quesnay and his followers lived in a country subject to political institutions, of which many were mischievous, more were imperfect, and all were unsettled. That the existing system of government was bad, every one acknowledged. The economists believed that they had discovered why it was bad. They believed that they had discovered that agriculture is the only source of wealth, and rent the only legitimate source of public revenue. And they proposed, therefore, to substitute for the innumerable taxes on importation, on exportation, on transit, on production, on sale, on consumption, and on the person of man, which then formed the fiscal system of France, a single tax on the rent of land. So far their precepts were founded on the science of Political Economy. But when they proposed the separation of legislative and judicial functions, and required the whole legislative power to center in an absolute hereditary monarch, they drew their premises from other branches of mental science. I have said that Turgot was an exception; and it is remarkable, that the only man among the disciples of Quesnay who was actually practising Political Economy as an art, is the only one who treated its principles as a science. His "Réflexions sur la Formation, et la Distribution des Richesses," published in 1771, is a purely scientific treatise. It contains not a word of precept; and might have been written by an ascetic, who believed wealth to be an evil.

We now come to Adam Smith, the founder of modern Political Economy, whether it be treated as a science or as an art. He considered it as an art. "Political Economy," he says, in the introduction to the fourth book, "proposes two distinct objects: first, to provide a plentiful revenue or subsistence for the people, or, more properly, to enable them to provide such a revenue or subsistence for themselves; and, secondly, to supply the state or common weal with a revenue sufficient for the public service. It proposes to enrich both the people and the sovereign." The principal purpose of his work was to show the erroneousness of the means by which political economists had proposed to attain these two great objects. And in the then state of knowledge, this could be done only by proving that many of them mistook the nature of wealth, and all of them the laws according to which it is produced and distributed. The scientific portion of his work is merely an introduction to that which is practical.

Of the five books into which the work is divided, it occupies only the first and second. The third is an historical sketch of the progress of national opulence. The fourth, the longest in the whole work, considers the direct interferences by which governments have attempted to lead or force their subjects to become rich; and decides, "that every system which endeavours, either by extraordinary encouragements, to draw towards a particular species of industry a greater share of the capital of the society than would naturally go to it, or, by extraordinary restraints, to force from a particular species of industry some share of the capital which would otherwise be employed in it, is in reality subversive of the great purpose which it means to promote. It retards, instead of accelerating, the progress of the society towards real wealth and greatness; and diminishes, instead of increasing, the real value of the annual produce of its land and labour."

"All systems," he adds, "either of preference or of restraint, therefore, being thus completely taken away, the obvious and simple system of natural liberty establishes itself of its own accord. According to that system, the sovereign has only three duties to attend to: first, the duty of protecting the society from the violence and invasion of other independent societies; secondly, the duty of protecting, as far as possible, every member of the society from the injustice or oppression of every other member of it, or the duty of establishing an exact administration of justice; and, thirdly, the duty of erecting and maintaining certain public works and certain public institutions, which it can never be for the interest of any individual, or small number of individuals, to erect and maintain."

The fifth book, which points out the means by which the duties of the sovereign may best be performed, and the necessary public revenue provided, is, in fact, a treatise on the art of government. It treats of the subsidiary arts of war, of jurisprudence, and of education. It considers the advantages and disadvantages of religious endowments, and even the details of the opposed systems of patronage and popular election, and of equality and inequality of benefices. It considers at great length the modes and effects of taxation and of public loans, and concludes by an elaborate plan for diminishing the taxation of Great Britain, by requiring all the British dependencies, of which Ireland and North America then formed part, to contribute directly to the imperial treasury.

I have often doubted whether we ought not to wish that Adam Smith had published his fifth book as a separate treatise with an appropriate title. It is by far the most amusing and the easiest portion of the "Wealth of Nations," and must have attracted many readers whom the abstractions of the first and second books, if they had formed a separate work, would have repelled. On the other hand, the including by so great an authority, in one treatise, and under one name, many subjects belonging to different arts, has certainly contributed to the indistinct views as to the nature and subjects of Political Economy, which appear still to prevail.

The English writers who have succeeded Adam Smith, have generally set out by defining Political Economy as a science, and proceeded to treat it as an art.

Thus Mr. M'Culloch states, as the proper subjects of Political Economy, "the laws which regulate the production, accumulation, distribution, and consumption of the articles or products possessing exchangeable value." Political Economy, then, is a science. But he goes on to say, that "the object of Political Economy is to point out the means by which the industry of man may be rendered most productive of wealth, the circumstances most favourable to its accumulation, and the mode in which it may be most advantageously consumed." So defined, Political Economy is an art,—a branch, in fact the principal branch, of the art of government.

Mr. James Mill says that he has in view merely to ascertain the laws of production, distribution, and consumption. His treatise, therefore, ought to be merely scientific. But when he says that Political Economy ought to be to the state what domestic economy is to the family, and that its object is to ascertain the means of multiplying the objects of desire, and to frame a system of rules for applying them with the greatest advantage to that end, he turns it into an art.

Mr. Ricardo is, however, an exception. His great work is little less scientific than that of Turgot. His abstinence from precept, and even from illustrations drawn from real life, is the more remarkable, as the subject of his treatise is distribution, the most practical branch of Political Economy, and taxation, the most practical branch of distribution.

The modern economists of France, Germany, Spain, Italy, and America, so far as I am acquainted with their works, all treat Political Economy as an art.

Many of them complain of what they call the abstractions of the English school, and others accuse it of narrow views, and of an exclusive attention to wealth; criticisms which must arise from an opinion that Political Economy is a branch of the art of government, and that its business is to influence the conduct of a statesman, rather than to extend the knowledge of a philosopher.

It appears, from this hasty sketch, that the term Political Economy has not yet acquired a definite meaning, and that, whichever of the three definitions I adopt, I shall be free from the accusation of having unduly extended or narrowed the field of inquiry which the statute founding this professorship has laid open to me.

There is much in favour of the third definition, that which defines Political Economy as the art which teaches what production, distribution, accumulation, and consumption of wealth is most conducive to the happiness of mankind, and what are the habits and institutions most favourable to that production, distribution, accumulation, and consumption.

It raises the political economist to a commanding eminence. The most extensive, though perhaps not the most important, portion of human nature, lies within his horizon.

The possession of wealth is the great object of human desire, its production is the great purpose of human exertion. The modes and the degree in which it is distributed, accumulated, and consumed, occasion the principal differences between nations. The philosopher who could teach such an art, would stand at the head of the benefactors of mankind.

But the subject is too vast for a single treatise, or indeed for a single mind. This will be evident if we consider the extent of one of its subordinate branches, the limits to be assigned to posthumous power. On the death of a proprietor, ought his property to revert to the state, as it does in Turkey, or to go to his children, as it does in France, or to be subject to his disposition by deed or by will? If it be subjected to his disposition, ought he to have merely the power of appointing his immediate successors, or of entailing it for one generation, or for two, or for ever? Is it advisable that he should have the power, not only of appointing a successor to his property, but of directing how that successor shall employ it? And ought such a power to be unlimited, or to be confined to certain purposes, or within a certain period? Ought the laws of succession and of testamentary power to be the same as respects land and movables, or to differ totally, or in any, or what, particulars? Ought these questions to be resolved differently in an old country and in a colony, in a monarchy, in an aristocracy, and in a republic? If Political Economy be a branch of the art of government, these inquiries form a branch, though a very small one, of Political Economy.

But there is scarcely any one of them which it would not require a long treatise to answer satisfactorily. How many, for instance, are the considerations which must be attended to in a discussion as to the propriety of enabling individuals to found permanent institutions for the purposes of religion, of education, and of charity, and as to the period for which they ought to be allowed to govern them from the grave?

It is almost impossible to overrate the importance of the art of government. With the exception, perhaps, of morality, it is the most useful of the mental arts; but, with no exception whatever, it is the most extensive. Too much attention cannot be given to it; but that attention should be subdivided. Too many minds cannot be employed on it, but each should select a single province; and the narrower the province, of course the more completely is it likely to be mastered.

My second definition, that which defines Political Economy as the art which teaches what are the institutions and habits most favourable to the production and accumulation of wealth, is not liable to similar objections. It opens a field of inquiry, positively indeed wide, but comparatively narrow. The object proposed by the political economist is no longer human happiness, but the attainment of one of the means of human happiness, wealth.

To recur to my former illustrations, he must, as in the former case, inquire whether, according to the principles of Political Economy, individuals ought to be enabled to direct how the property which they have acquired in life shall be employed after their deaths, in providing religious teaching, and to what extent, and for what periods, their posthumous legislation ought to be enforced; but he must stop far short of the point to which his inquiries, if he had adopted the former definition, would have extended. He must confine himself to the effect of such institutions on the production and accumulation of wealth. He has now no business to inquire whether endowments imply articles of faith, and articles of faith produce indifference or hypocrisy; whether the servility of a hierarchy be compensated by its loyalty, or the turbulence of sectarianism by its independence of thought. He has no longer to compare the moral and religious influence of an endowed, with that of an unendowed clergy. He does not inquire whether the morality of the one is likely to be ascetic, and that of the other latitudinarian; whether the one will have more influence over the bulk of the people, and the other over the educated classes; whether the one is likely to produce numerous contending sects, animated by zeal, but inflamed by intolerance, and the other an unreflecting apathetic conformity. These are matters beyond his jurisdiction. But he assumes, on the general principles of human nature, that every civilised society requires teachers of religion, and that these teachers must be paid for their services. He shows, on the principles of Political Economy, that in every such society there are revenues derived from land or from capital, which are consumed by a class not forced to take an active part in producing them, and enjoying, therefore, a leisure which they are tempted to waste in indolence or in frivolous occupation. He shows that to dedicate a portion of these revenues to the payment of the teachers of religion, is merely to substitute for a certain number of lay landlords, or lay fundholders, bound to the performance of no public duty, ecclesiastical fundholders, or ecclesiastical landlords, rendering, in return for their incomes, services which, under what is called the voluntary system, must be purchased by those who require them. He shows that such a dedication must diminish the number of idle persons, and therefore increase the productive activity of the community and diminish the subjects of necessary expenditure, and therefore increase its disposable income; and he infers that the wealth of a society may be augmented by allowing such endowments to be created. He may go on to show that such endowments may cease to be favourable to wealth, if the founder's legislative power be unlimited, since the doctrines of which he has ordered the dissemination may have been originally unpopular, or may become so as knowledge advances. The political economist, therefore, may recommend that all such institutions be subjected to the control of the legislature, in order to prevent endowments from being wasted by providing teachers for whom there are no congregations, and that they be also subjected to periodical revision, in order to accommodate the supply of instruction to the demand.

He may proceed to consider the different forms of endowments, by tithes, by land, by rent-charges, and by the investment of money. He may show how the first is an obstacle to all improvement, and the second to improvement by the landlord; how the third diminishes with the progress of wealth, and the fourth may perish with the fund on which it is secured. And he may propose remedies for these different inconveniences. If he go further than this, he wanders from the art of wealth into the art of government.

I have introduced this rather long illustration, not only as an example of the different modes in which the *art* of Political Economy must be treated, according to the definition with which the teacher sets out, but also as a specimen of the extent and variety of the details into which he must enter, even if he adopt the less extensive definition.

But this is not all. I have already remarked that all the practical arts draw their principles from sciences. If, however, the teacher of an art were to attempt to teach also the different sciences on which it is founded, his treatise would want unity of subject, and be inconveniently long. He generally, therefore, assumes his scientific principles as established, and refers to them as well known. The teacher of the art of medicine merely alludes to the facts which form the sciences of anatomy and chemistry; the teacher of rhetoric assumes that his pupil is acquainted with the science of logic and with that of grammar. Many of the sciences and of the arts which are subservient to the art of Political Economy, may be thus treated. The political economist, for instance, assumes that protection from domestic or foreign violence or fraud, is essential to any considerable production or accumulation of wealth, and he considers the means by which the expense of providing this protection may be best supported; but he does not inquire what are the necessary legal and military institutions. He leaves these to be pointed out by the arts of war and of penal and civil jurisprudence, and by the sciences on which those arts depend.

There is one science, however, to which this treatment cannot as yet be applied, and it is the science most intimately connected with the art of Political Economy, that is to say, the science which states the laws regulating the production, accumulation, and distribution of wealth, or, in other words, the science (as distinguished from the art) of Political Economy itself. The time I trust will come, perhaps within the lives of some of us, when the outline of this science will be clearly made out and generally recognised, when its nomenclature will be fixed, and its principles form a part of elementary instruction. A teacher of the art of Political Economy will then be able to refer to the principles of the science as familiar and admitted truths. I scarcely need repeat how far this is from being the case at present. Without doubt, many of the laws of the science have been discovered, and a few of them are generally acknowledged; and some of its terms have been defined, and the definitions accepted. Still, however, there remains, as I remarked in the first Lecture, much to explore and much to explain. We are still far from the bounds of what is to be known, and further still from any general agreement as to what is known. Every writer, therefore, on the art of Political Economy, is forced to prefix, or to interweave among his precepts, his own views of the science, and thus to add to the practical portion of his work a scientific portion of perhaps equal length. It appears to me, that the five years during which this professorship is tenable, is too short a period for so vast an undertaking. I propose, therefore, to take as my subject, not the art, but the much narrower province, the science; and to explain, in the following Lectures, the general laws which regulate the production, accumulation, and distribution of wealth, leaving it to writers with more leisure to point out what are the institutions most favourable to its production and accumulation, and to speculators of still wider views to say what production, accumulation, distribution, and consumption are most favourable to human happiness.

But though I follow substantially the example of Turgot and Ricardo, I do not propose to follow it implicitly. Though I profess to teach only the theory of wealth, I do not refuse the right to consider its practical application. There is, indeed, something imposing and almost seductive in a work of pure science, especially if it be a science connected with human affairs. We admire the impartiality of the philosopher who discusses matters that agitate nations without mixing in the strife, or noticing the use that may be made of the truths which he scatters. And we admit, with comparative readiness, conclusions which do not appear to have been influenced by passion, the great disturber of observation and of reasoning. This was one of the great causes of the popularity of Ricardo. He was the first English writer who produced Political Economy in a purely scientific form. He is usually a logical reasoner, so that his conclusions can seldom be denied if his premises are conceded, and his premises must usually be conceded, for they are usually hypothetical. Men were delighted to find what appeared to be firm footing, in a new and apparently unstable science, and readily gave their assent to theories which did not obviously lead to practice. But though it be desirable that from time to time a writer should arise able and willing to treat the science in this severe and abstract manner, his treatise will be more serviceable to masters than to students. To those who are already familiar with the subject, to those who have already perceived how deeply mankind are interested in obtaining correct views as to the laws which regulate the production and distribution of wealth, a naked statement of those laws, though it should not possess the elegance of Turgot, or the originality of Ricardo, must still be useful, and even agreeable. A mere student would find it repulsive. He ought to be attracted to Political Economy by seeing from time to time its practical application. He should be taught that he is studying a science composed of principles which no statesman, no legislator, no magistrate, no member even of a board of guardians can safely disregard. And this will be best effected by putting before him examples of the good which has been done by adhering to those principles, and of the evil which has punished their neglect. These examples, therefore, I shall think myself at liberty to give. I shall think myself justified, for instance, in showing how the natural distribution of wealth may be affected by the institution of poor-laws. And I shall not confine myself to their effects upon wealth. I shall consider how far a well-framed poor-law may promote the moral as well as the material welfare of the labouring classes, and an ill-administered poor-law may produce moral, intellectual, and physical degradation. But these discussions must be considered as episodes. They form no part of the science which I profess. I shall enter into them, not as a political economist, but as a statesman or a moralist; and I shall expect from those who do me the honour of listening to them, not the full conviction which follows scientific reasoning, but the qualified assent which is given to the precepts of an art.

In the next Lecture I shall consider whether the science of Political Economy may be more conveniently based on positive or on hypothetical principles.

LECTURE IV
THAT POLITICAL ECONOMY IS A POSITIVE, NOT AN HYPOTHETICAL SCIENCE.—DEFINITION OF WEALTH

In the present Lecture I shall consider whether the science of Political Economy may be more conveniently based on positive or on hypothetical principles, and shall afterwards explain, more fully than I have as yet done, the sense in which I use the word wealth. Mr. John Mill, who has contributed much to Political Economy, as he has, indeed, to every science which he has touched, maintains that it is based on hypothesis. As it is impossible to change Mr. Mill's language for the better, I shall extract the material parts of the passage in which he states and supports this opinion.

"Political Economy,"[D] he says, "is concerned with man solely as a being who desires to possess wealth, and who is capable of judging of the comparative efficacy of means for obtaining that end. It predicts only such of the phenomena of the social state as take place in consequence of the pursuit of wealth. It makes entire abstraction of every other human passion or motive, except those which may be regarded as perpetually antagonising principles to the desire of wealth; namely, aversion to labour, and desire of the present enjoyment of costly indulgences. These it takes, to a certain extent, into its calculations, because these do not merely, like other desires, occasionally conflict with the pursuit of wealth, but accompany it always as a drag or impediment, and are therefore inseparably mixed up in the consideration of it. Political Economy considers mankind as occupied solely in acquiring and consuming wealth, and aims at showing what is the course of action into which mankind, living in a state of society, would be impelled, if that motive, except in the degree in which it is checked by the two perpetual counter-motives above adverted to, were absolutely ruler of all their actions. Under the influence of this desire, it shows mankind accumulating wealth, and employing wealth in the production of other wealth; sanctioning by mutual agreement the institution of property; establishing laws to prevent individuals from encroaching upon the property of others by force or fraud; adopting various contrivances for increasing the productiveness of their labour; settling the division of the produce by agreement, under the influence of competition (competition itself being governed by certain laws, which laws are therefore the ultimate regulators of the division of the produce), and employing certain expedients, as money, credit, &c., to facilitate the distribution. All these operations, though many of them are really the result of a plurality of motives, are considered by Political Economy as flowing solely from the desire of wealth. The science then proceeds to investigate the laws which govern these several operations, under the supposition that man is a being who is determined, by the necessity of his nature, to prefer a greater proportion of wealth to a smaller in all cases, without any other exception than that constituted by the two counter-motives already specified. Not that any political economist was ever so absurd as to suppose that mankind are really thus constituted, but because this is the mode in which science must necessarily proceed. When an effect depends upon a concurrence of causes, those causes must be studied one at a time, and their laws separately investigated, if we wish, through the causes, to obtain the power of either predicting or controlling the effect; since the law of the effect is compounded of the laws of all the causes which determine it. The law of the centripetal and that of the tangential force must have been known, before the motions of the earth and planets could be explained, or many of them predicted. The same is the case with the conduct of man in society. In order to judge how he will act under the variety of desires and aversions which are concurrently operating upon him, we must know how he would act under the exclusive influence of each one in particular. There is, perhaps, no action of a man's life in which he is neither under the immediate nor under the remote influence of any impulse but the mere desire of wealth. With respect to those parts of human conduct of which wealth is not even the principal object, to these Political Economy does not pretend that its conclusions are applicable. But there are also certain departments of human affairs, in which the acquisition of wealth is the main and acknowledged end. It is only of these that Political Economy takes notice. The manner in which it necessarily proceeds is that of treating the main and acknowledged end as if it were the sole end; which, of all hypotheses equally simple, is the nearest to the truth. The political economist inquires, what are the actions which would be produced by this desire, if, within the departments in question, it were unimpeded by any other?

> [D] Essays on some Unsettled Questions of Political
> Economy, pp. 137, 138, 139, 140, 144, 145.

"It reasons, and, as we contend, must necessarily reason, from assumptions, not from facts. It is built upon hypotheses strictly analogous to those which, under the name of definitions, are the foundation of the other abstract sciences. Geometry presupposes an arbitrary definition of a line, 'that which has length but not breadth.' Just in the same manner does Political Economy presuppose an arbitrary definition of man, as a being who invariably does that by which he may obtain the greatest amount of necessaries, conveniences, and luxuries, with the smallest quantity of labour and physical self-denial with which they can be obtained in the existing state of knowledge. It is true that this definition of man is not formally prefixed to any work on Political Economy, as the definition of a line is prefixed to Euclid's Elements; and in proportion as, by being so prefixed, it would be less in danger of being forgotten, we may see ground for regret that it is not done. It is proper that what is assumed in every particular case, should once for all be brought before the mind in its full extent, by being somewhere formally stated as a general maxim. Now, no one who is conversant with systematic treatises on Political Economy will question, that whenever a political economist has shown that, by acting in a particular manner, a labourer may obviously obtain higher wages, a capitalist larger profits, or a landlord higher rent, he concludes, as a matter of course, that they will certainly act in that manner. Political Economy, therefore, reasons from assumed premises—from premises which might be totally without foundation in fact, and which are not pretended to be universally in accordance with it. The conclusions of Political Economy, consequently, like those of geometry, are only true, as the common phrase is, in the abstract; that is, they are only true under certain suppositions, in which none but general causes—causes common to the whole class of cases under consideration—are taken into account."

I have extracted this long passage because it is a clear statement of an original view of the science of Political Economy,—a view so plausible, indeed so philosophical, that I feel bound either to adopt it, or to state fully my reasons for rejecting it. I am not aware of any writer, except, perhaps, Mr. Merivale, who has expressed a formal concurrence in Mr. Mill's doctrine; but Mr. Ricardo has practically assented to it.

His treatment of the science, indeed, is still more abstract than that proposed by Mr. Mill. He adds to Mr. Mill's hypothesis other assumptions equally arbitrary; and he draws all his illustrations, not from real life, but from hypothetical cases. Out of these materials he has framed a theory, as to the distribution of wealth, possessing almost mathematical precision.

But neither the reasoning of Mr. Mill, nor the example of Mr. Ricardo, induce me to treat Political Economy as an hypothetical science. I do not think it necessary, and, if unnecessary, I do not think it desirable.

It appears to me, that if we substitute for Mr. Mill's hypothesis, that wealth and costly enjoyment are the *only* objects of human desire, the statement that they are universal and constant objects of desire, that they are desired by all men and at all times, we shall have laid an equally firm foundation for our subsequent reasonings, and have put a truth in the place of an arbitrary assumption. We shall not, it is true, from the fact that by acting in a particular manner a labourer may obtain higher wages, a capitalist larger profits, or a landlord higher rent, be able to infer the further fact that they will certainly act in that manner, but we shall be able to infer that they will do so in the absence of disturbing causes. And if we are able, as will frequently be the case, to state the cases in which these causes may be expected to exist, and the force with which they are likely to operate, we shall have removed all objection to the positive as opposed to the hypothetical treatment of the science.

I have said that the hypothetical treatment of the science, if unnecessary, is undesirable. It appears to me to be open to three great objections. In the first place it is obviously unattractive. No one listens to an exposition of what might be the state of things under given but unreal conditions, with the interest with which he hears a statement of what is actually taking place.

In the second place, a writer who starts from arbitrarily assumed premises, is in danger of forgetting, from time to time, their unsubstantial foundation, and of arguing as if they were true. This has been the source of much error in Ricardo. He assumed the land of every country to be of different degrees of fertility, and rent to be the value of the difference between the fertility of the best and of the worst land in cultivation. The remainder of the produce he divided into profit and wages. He assumed that wages naturally amount to neither more nor less than the amount of commodities which nature or habit has rendered necessary to maintain the labourer and his family in health and strength. He assumed that, in the progress of population and wealth, worse and worse soils are constantly resorted to, and that agricultural labour, therefore, becomes less and less proportionately productive; and he inferred that the share of the produce of land taken by the landlord and by the labourer must constantly increase, and the share taken by the capitalist constantly diminish.

This was a logical inference, and would consequently have been true in fact, if the assumed premises had been true. The fact is, however, that almost every one of them is false. It is not true that rent depends on the difference in fertility of the different portions of land in cultivation. It might exist if the whole territory of a country were of uniform quality. It is not true that the labourer always receives precisely the necessaries, or even what custom leads him to consider the necessaries, of life. In civilised countries he almost always receives much more; in barbarous countries he from time to time obtains less. It is not true that as wealth and population advance, agricultural labour becomes less and less proportionately productive. The corn now raised with the greatest labour in England is raised with less labour than that which was raised with the least labour three hundred years ago, or than that which is now raised with the least labour in Poland. It is not true that the share of the produce taken by the capitalist is least in the richest countries. Those are the countries in which it generally is the greatest. Mr. Ricardo was certainly justified in assuming his premises, provided that he was always aware, and always kept in mind, that they were merely assumed. This, however, he seems sometimes not to know, and sometimes he forgets. Thus he states, as an actual fact, that in an improving country, the difficulty of obtaining raw produce constantly increases. He states as a real fact, that a tax on wages falls not on the labourer but on the capitalist.

He affirms that tithes occasion a proportionate increase in the price of corn, and a proportionate increase of wages, and therefore are a tax on the capitalist, not on the landlord. Positions both of which depend on an assumed fixed amount of wages.

A third objection to reasoning on hypothesis is its liability to error, either from illogical inference, or from the omission of some element necessarily incident to the supposed case. When a writer takes his premises from observation and consciousness, and infers from them what he supposes to be real facts, if he have committed any grave error, it generally leads him to some startling conclusion. He is thus warned of the probable existence of an unfounded premise, or of an illogical inference, and if he be wise, tries back until he has detected his mistake. But the strangeness of the results of an hypothesis, gives no warning. We expect them to differ from what we observe, and lose, therefore, this incidental means of testing the correctness of our reasoning.

An illustration of this may be found in the eminently ingenious and eminently erroneous work of Colonel Torrens, called "The Budget." Colonel Torrens supposes the commercial world to consist of only two countries, equal in wealth and civilisation, which he calls England and Cuba. He supposes that England has peculiar advantages for the production of woollens, and Cuba for that of sugar, and that the cloth of the one, and the sugar of the other, are freely exchanged in proportion to the labour which each has cost. He then supposes Cuba to impose a duty on English cloth, which would of course, to a certain extent, prevent its importation; and he states that the consequence would be, that England would have to send money to Cuba for sugar, until the exportation of money had impoverished England, and its importation had enriched Cuba.

Now if Colonel Torrens, instead of hypothetical, had taken real cases, if he had inquired, for instance, into the results of the prohibitive system of France, and had come to the conclusion that that system increases her wealth, the strangeness of such a result would have led him to suspect an error in his facts or in his reasoning. But the strangeness of the result of an imaginary case did not rouse his suspicion. The fact is, that his hypothetical argument is erroneous; and the error consists in his not having taken into account an element essentially incident to his supposed case, namely, the influence of commercial restrictions on the efficiency of labour. If he had taken this element into account, he would have found that Cuba, by her prohibitive system, would diminish the productive power of her labour, and consequently would find it her interest to import from England commodities which she previously produced at home; so that the ultimate result would probably be, rather an export of gold from Cuba than from England.

Colonel Torrens's book always reminds me of the suit of clothes which the Laputa tailor cut on hypothetical data. Unfortunately, however, for the credit of the Laputa artist, Gulliver tried them on, and the error which had slipped into the calculation showed itself in every form of misfit. Happily for Colonel Torrens, and happily for ourselves, we have not tried on his theory.

But though the objections against founding the science on hypothesis seem to me decisive, I do not give up hypothetical illustrations. Such illustrations not only make abstract reasonings more easily intelligible, they often expose their errors. Conclusions which appeared to be correct, when the vague terms of capital and labour, profit and wages, were used, are often found to be erroneous, when an hypothetical example embodies these abstractions, and endeavours to show the moral and physical processes by which the supposed result would be obtained. The absence of such illustrations is one of the great defects of Adam Smith. Perhaps this very defect contributed to the popularity of his work. Such illustrations, however useful, always give an appearance of stiffness and pedantry. The careless reader or hearer neglects them, and the real student is annoyed at having to learn the *dramatis personæ* of an imaginary case. But if Smith had used them, he would probably have avoided some errors, and have preserved his successors from many more. His example in this and in some other respects, introduced a loose, popular mode of treating Political Economy, which has mainly retarded its progress.

It may be remarked, that I have as yet used the word wealth, without defining it. I have done so, because I employ it in its popular sense, and because the ideas usually attached to that word appear to me to be sufficiently precise, to prevent any danger of my hearers misunderstanding it. Having now, however, completed the introduction to the science of Political Economy, having marked out its province, and stated the mode in which I intend to treat it, I think it advisable formally to define the term which expresses its subject matter. And this for two reasons. First, because, in a scientific work, every technical term ought to be defined; and, secondly, because that term has been employed by many of those who have preceded me, in senses differing from that which I adopt.

In ordinary use, and I think it is the most convenient use, wealth comprehends all those things, and those things only, which, directly or indirectly, are made the subjects of purchase and sale, of letting and hiring. For this purpose, they must, in the first place, possess utility, or, in other words, be capable of affording pleasure or preventing pain, since no one would purchase or hire anything absolutely useless. In the second place, they must be limited in supply, since no one would buy anything of which he might acquire as much as he pleased by merely taking possession of it. The water in the open sea is practically unlimited in supply; any one who chooses to go for it, may have as much of it as he pleases. The portion of it which has been brought to London to supply salt water baths is limited, and cannot be obtained, therefore, without payment. In the third place, nothing is wealth that is not capable of appropriation. Fine weather is useful, and is limited in supply, but it is not wealth, since it cannot be appropriated. Some things are capable of appropriation only under peculiar circumstances. In an extensive, thinly inhabited plain, light and air are incapable of appropriation, every inhabitant may enjoy them equally; but in a town, one house intercepts them from another. A town house, surrounded by an open space, has more of them than one in a street. The possessor of such a house, and of the ground which surrounds it, has practically appropriated its peculiar advantages of light and air; they add to its value, and form, therefore, part of his wealth. He even may sell them without parting with his house, by selling the privilege of erecting buildings which will intercept them. Fourthly, as is implied by the definition, nothing can be wealth which is not directly or indirectly transferable. High birth is agreeable and rare, it may add to the happiness of its possessor, but, as it is absolutely incapable of transfer, it is not part of his wealth. Most of our personal qualities are only indirectly transferable; they are transferable, not in themselves, but embodied in the commodities which their possessor can produce, or in the services which he can render. The skill of a painter is transferable in the form of a commodity, his pictures; the skill of a surgeon in that of a service, the dexterity with which he performs an operation. Such qualities perish by the death of the possessor, or may be impaired or destroyed by disease, or rendered valueless by changes in the customs of the country, which put an end to the demand for their products. Even to the same person, and under the same circumstances in all other respects, they may become wealth, or cease to be wealth, merely in consequence of a change in the social position of their possessor. When Miss Linley became Mrs. Sheridan, her powers of action and song ceased to be wealth; they remained the delight of private societies, but were no longer objects of sale. If Sheridan had condescended to accept an income on such terms, his wife's accomplishments would have enriched him. Subject, however, to these contingencies, personal qualities are wealth, and wealth of the most valuable kind. The amount of the revenue derived from their exercise in England, far exceeds the rental of all its land.

The words wealth and value differ as substance and attribute. All those things, and those things only, which constitute wealth, are valuable. As the meaning of the term value has been the subject of long and eager controversy, I shall, at a future period, consider at some length the different significations which have been given to it. It is enough to say at present that I use it in its popular acceptation, as signifying in anything the quality which fits it to be given and received in exchange, or, in other words, to be let or sold, hired or purchased.

It follows, from this definition of wealth, that in a community enjoying perfect abundance, there would be no wealth. If every object of desire could be procured by a wish, nothing would have value, and nothing would be exchanged. It follows, also, that it is possible to conceive at least a temporary diminution of the wealth of a community occasioned by an increase of their means of enjoyment. This would be the immediate consequence of any cause which should occasion the supply of any useful article to change from limited to unlimited. Thus, if the climate of England could suddenly be changed to that of Bogota, and the warmth which we extract imperfectly and expensively from fuel were supplied by the sun, fuel would cease to be useful, except as one of the productive instruments employed by art. We should want no more grates or chimney-pieces in our sitting-rooms. What had previously been a considerable amount of property in the fixtures of houses, in stock in trade, and materials, would become valueless. Coals would sink in price; the most expensive mines would be abandoned; those which were retained would afford smaller rents. The proprietors and tradesmen specially affected by the change would lose not only in wealth, but in the means of enjoyment. The owner of a mine whose rent fell from 20,000*l.* a year to 10,000*l.*, would not be compensated by being saved the expense of fuel in every room except his kitchen. On the other hand, persons without fire-places or coal-cellars of their own, would lose nothing, and the rest of the world would lose only in the value of their grates, chimney-pieces, and stocks of coal; and all would gain in enjoyment by being able to devote to other purposes the money which they previously paid for artificial warmth. Still for a time there would be less wealth. That time, indeed, would be short; the capital and the labour previously devoted to warming our apartments, would be diverted to the production of new commodities. The cheapness of coal would increase the supply of manufactured articles, and there would then be as much wealth as there was before the change; probably more, and certainly much more enjoyment. It is probable that salt forms a smaller part of the wealth of England than of Hindostan, though every Englishman has twenty times as much of it as every Hindoo. The Englishman is allowed to use freely the abundant supply offered by nature. In Hindostan there is a natural scarcity, aggravated tenfold by the Government.

We may conceive a case in which unlimited abundance would destroy not only the value, but the utility of a whole class of commodities; would prevent them not merely from being objects of exchange, but even from being objects of desire. This would be the case as to all the commodities whose only utility is to be a means of displaying wealth. If emeralds were suddenly to become as abundant as pebbles, they could be no longer used as ornaments; and if no other use could be made of them, and I am not aware of any, they would be valueless. All their possessors, at the time of the change, would find themselves poorer, and neither they nor any one else would be compensated by any increased means of enjoyment. It would be a mere destruction of wealth.

It may be as well to remark, that things may be wealth to individuals without forming part of the wealth of the community to which those individuals belong. This is the case with respect to almost all the wealth created by an artificial limitation of supply. The monopolies with which Elizabeth rewarded her favourites were wealth to them, but diminished the wealth of the rest of the community. The same may be said of a patent right, or of the secrecy of a manufacturing process. The process itself, which is protected by the patent or by the secrecy, is part of the wealth of the community, since it enables them to have more or better commodities; but the monopoly granted by the patent, or guarded by the secrecy, is wealth only to its owner. As soon as the patent terminates, or the secret is divulged, the wealth of the community is increased by the increased abundance of the commodities to the production of which every one may now apply the process.

Again, the national debt is wealth to the proprietors of stock, but as the sum received in dividends is paid in taxes, it cannot form a part of the wealth of the nation. If, indeed, those two sums precisely coincided, if there were no expenses of collection, and if taxes did not interfere with the production of wealth, the national debt would not diminish the national wealth, though it could not augment it. It would be a mere matter of distribution. But the expense of collecting the national revenue, and the interference of taxation with production, are so much pure loss; and by the amount of these two sources of expense and loss, we should be richer if the national debt were repudiated.

The wealth which consists merely of a right or credit on the part of A. with a corresponding duty or debt on the part of B., is not considered by the political economist. He deals with the things which are the subjects of the right or of the credit, not with the claims or the liabilities which may affect them. In fact, the credit amounts merely to this, that B. has in his hands a part of the property of A.

I have said that my definition of wealth differs from that which has been adopted by many of my predecessors. Some political economists extend the term to all the objects of human desire; others restrict it to what they have called material products; and others to the things which cannot be acquired or produced without labour. The objections to the first definition are obvious. If wealth be the subject of Political Economy, and wealth include all that man desires, Political Economy, whether a science or an art, is the science or the art which treats of human happiness—a subject, as I have already remarked, too extensive to be included in a single treatise. The second, that which confines wealth to material objects, is more plausible. It includes all visible wealth, it includes all wealth which is capable of direct and complete sale. The things which it excludes are mere objects of the intellect. They may be shared, but cannot be completely transferred, since the proprietor, though he may impart them, cannot divest himself of them; they may produce permanent effects, but perish themselves with the individual mind of which they are qualities. But as they obey, in other respects, the same laws as material wealth, are obtained by the same means, and owe their value to the same causes, I think their exclusion a fatal objection to a definition of wealth. The definition which confines wealth to the things which cannot be acquired or produced without labour, differs little from mine, which confines it to things limited in supply. Whatever must be obtained by labour is necessarily limited in supply, the supply of labour itself being limited; and, on the other hand, there are, in fact, scarcely any, if there be any, commodities limited in supply and capable of transfer, which can be obtained without some labour. So that wealth is always found subject to both these incidents. Nor does value appear to depend on either incident exclusively. A quarter of corn from the best, and one from the worst land, of equal goodness, sell in the same market at the same price, though one may have cost three times as much labour as the other. The pictures of Hans

Hemling are far more limited in supply than those of Raffaelle, and yet they sell for much less.

We can separate, however, the two qualities in our minds. We can suppose a commodity useful and transferable to be limited in supply, but that supply to be gratuitously afforded by nature. About 1,980,000 lbs. weight of silver is supposed to be now annually supplied. Now, if precisely the same quantity of pure silver as is now produced daily in each refining house, were every day to be supernaturally deposited on a table in the refining house, and all other sources of supply were to cease, silver would continue to be limited in supply just as it is now, but would no longer be procured by labour. Is there any reason for supposing that its value would alter? If its value would remain the same, it follows that it depends on limitation of supply, and that limitation of supply, not the necessity of labour, is the differentia which constitutes wealth. An uncut copy of an early printed book is worth, perhaps, ten times as much as a copy which has been fitted to be read by cutting open its leaves. Because it has cost more labour? No: it has cost rather less. Because it is more readable? No: it is useless for the purpose of reading. Simply because such copies are more limited in supply.